PIERO DELLA FRANCESCA

ALBERTO BUSIGNANI

GROSSET & DUNLAP
Publishers - New York

First American edition published 1968 by Grosset & Dunlap, Inc.

All rights reserved

Translated from the Italian by Pearl Sanders
Translation copyright © 1968 by Thames & Hudson, London
Copyright © 1967 by Sadea Editore, Firenze
Library of Congress Catalog Card Number 68-26682

Printed and bound in Italy

Life

Little has come down to us in the form of documents relating to the life of Piero della Francesca, so that in order to reconstruct the course of his life we must rely on the information we can glean from the works themselves and their impact on the art of Northern and Central Italy, in relation to which Piero was the second father of the Renaissance.[1]

He was born between 1410 and 1420, probably closer to the latter date. The first record in which his name appears occurs in a document of the Hospital of Santa Maria Nuova, Florence, regarding payments made to Domenico Veneziano for frescoes in the choir of Sant'Egidio, and dated 7 September 1439: 'Pietro di Benedetto of Borgo San Sepolcro is with him'. It would not be too far-fetched to assume from this that the first meeting between Piero and Domenico took place a few years earlier, perhaps about 1435 as Longhi suggests, and that the young apprentice followed Domenico Veneziano (who came from Florence, in spite of the name he was given) to his home in Umbria, referred to in a letter of 1438 to Piero de' Medici. Alternatively, Domenico may have discovered him on his return journey to Florence, or even earlier during his travels in Tuscany, Umbria and the Marches (it may possibly be to this early period in the relations between them that Vasari's mention of the collaboration of the two artists at Loreto refers). Domenico's discovery of the unknown young artist might well have occurred at a time when Piero was engaged in grinding colours for Antonio d'Anghiari, who had signed a contract in 1430 to produce a painting for the high altar of the church of San Francesco at Borgo.

However the two artists first met, it was certainly not chance alone which drew them together, except perhaps in the initial stages, since the speculation which surely occupied the young artist at the time can only have coincided exactly with the conclusions Domenico was then drawing from the work of Masaccio.

In 1442, three years after the record referring to Piero's presence in Florence, he was elected a town councillor at Borgo San Sepolcro, and in 1445, again at Borgo, the Brotherhood of Mercy (*Confraternità della Misericordia*) commissioned him to paint a polyptych for their altar, specifying that it was to be completed by 1448. Piero must have visited Urbino for the first time during the years immediately following if, as would appear likely from close stylistic similarities, the *Flagellation of Christ* is to be placed among the small group of works painted in the same period, or even before the earliest part of the *Polyptych of the Misericordia* (*Baptism of Christ,* London; *St Jerome,* Venice) and close in time to the violent death in 1444 of Oddantonio da Montefeltro, who has been recognized from earliest times in the figure of the youth shown on the right of the painting. From Urbino to Ferrara (1449) and to Rimini (1451), Piero's journeys followed closely on those of Alberti, who would probably not have failed to speak to both Lionello d'Este and Malatesta in praise of a painter so congenial to himself: Piero's travels through Emilia and Venetia influenced local painting, from the miniature-painters of the Borso d'Este Bible to Mantegna, Tura and Cossa, not to mention the Lendinaras — the extent of this influence is now stylistically documented history, and there is no need to dwell on it here.

When the Florentine artist Bicci di Lorenzo died in 1452, he had completed only a small part of the decoration of the choir of San Francesco in Arezzo. This was probably the date of Piero's arrival at Arezzo to carry on the work. ' Common sense suggests ', writes Longhi, ' that if a long interval in the work had elapsed, there would surely have been some artist of equal standing to Bicci di Lorenzo who could have completed the few parts he left unfinished in the ceiling and archway at the entrance to the choir, and taken care of the remainder, whereas even these small gaps can be seen to have been filled by Piero himself; this seems to be confirmed by his Rimini fresco, which was painted in 1451 and is already as bold, integrated and mature as the frescoes in Arezzo.'

4

The work at Arezzo lasted seven or eight years: during this time we know that Piero entered into a contract to produce an altarpiece for the high altar of the church of Sant'Agostino in Borgo (1459), to be completed within eight years, and that he probably travelled to Rome (as recorded by Vasari) to the court of Pope Nicholas V, who died in 1455; it was during this stay in Rome that he is believed by Longhi to have painted the fresco in Santa Maria Maggiore of which the *St Luke* remains.

By 1466, as evidenced by the document published by Milanesi[2] regarding the commission to Piero to paint the banner of the Company of the Annunciation (*Compagnia della Nunziata*) in Arezzo, the San Francesco frescoes in the same city were not only complete, but described as bringing glory to the artist. From this it seems probable that the scaffolding was removed as early as 1459, when Piero was paid in Rome for ' certain paintings... in the room of His Holiness, our Lord the Pope'. It was not a matter of chance that this Pope was Pius II, a confirmed believer in the theories of Leone Battista Alberti.

The question of which Roman paintings were by Piero's hand is rather complex: according to Vasari, he painted two cycles in the Vatican, while in the same author's later *Life* of Raphael mention is made of only one, of which, moreover, we have no other record. The problem remains insoluble even today, except from what might be inferred by looking at Melozzo da Forlì's famous fresco in the Vatican Library, which, in its monumentality and architectonic conception, is close to the art of Piero.

In 1462, Piero's brother Marco di Benedetto received from the Brotherhood of Mercy of Borgo the sum of fifteen crowns ' in part payment of the panel painted by M. Pietro his brother', who was no doubt away in Urbino or Arezzo. Stylistic disparities in the various parts of the Borgo polyptych are so great that it seems likely work had continued on it until this date; this supposition is reinforced by the tentative style of painting in, for example, the saints in the second row.

Piero returned to Borgo in 1466, and in 1467 was appointed to various public offices; in 1468 he was at

Bastia, near Borgo, where he had fled from the plague and was completing the *Nunziata* banner, handed over to the Brotherhood on 7 November of that year.

In 1469 he returned to Urbino and stayed at the house of Raphael's father, Giovanni Santi, to whom the Brotherhood of Corpus Domini refunded the sum of ten *bolognini* ' to pay the expenses of master Piero of Borgo who had come to see the panel in order to do it.' [3]

Back in Borgo, he was paid in 1469 by the friars of Sant'Agostino for the *St Augustine Polyptych* commissioned as long before as 1454, while a reference to his slowness in 1471, a power of attorney to his brother in 1473, and finally payment for the (lost) frescoes in the Chapel of the Madonna in the Badia (Abbey) Church on 12 April 1474 attest to his continued presence in his home town.

At this point references to him in Borgo documents cease for four years, a probable indication of a further journey to Urbino to paint the *Sinigallia Madonna* and the *Brera Altarpiece;* in Borgo in 1478 the Brotherhood of Mercy asked Piero to produce a fresco of the Virgin to be painted on a wall ' between the Church and the Hospital', but no other record of this fresco remains. In 1480 Piero was head of the Brotherhood of St Bartholomew, while in the same year the municipality began the work of restoring the wall on which he had painted the *Resurrection* a quarter of a century previously.

These were now the last years of Pietro's activity, although he went to Rimini in 1482, probably to begin a work of long duration, since he rented a house with the use of the garden and well: if nothing came of it, as seems likely from the complete lack of any record apart from the rental of the house from Giacosa, widow of Ganimede Borelli, this is probably due not so much to his old age as to the blindness of which Vasari speaks, and which is confirmed by a moving testimony by one Marco of Longaro, quoted in the memoirs of Berto degli Alberti: ' When this Marco was a boy, he led by the hand master Piero della Francesca, an excellent painter, who had gone blind; so much he told me.'

Five years later, the will drawn up by Ser Lionardo, the son of that Ser Marco Fedeli who in 1445 had prepared the contract for the *Polyptych of the Misericordia,* read as follows:

' I wish to be buried in the Abbey in our cemetery. I leave for the poor of the Abbey ten lire and leave to the body of Christ ten lire and to the Madonna of the Abbey ten lire and ten lire to the Madonna of la Reghia and of the remainder of my goods I leave half to my brother Antonio and if Antonio dies before me to his sons and the other half to the sons of Marco namely Francesco Bastiano and Girolamo and if one of them dies his share should go to the other.'

Finally, in Book III of the dead of the Brotherhood of St Bartholomew of Borgo San Sepolcro, we read: ' M. Piero di Benedetto de' Franceschi famous painter, on 12 October 1492; buried in the Abbey.'

Works

It is probable that at the time when Domenico Veneziano was completing his work on the frescoes in the choir of Sant'Egidio, and the twenty-year old artist from Borgo was ' with him ', the painting Piero della Francesca studied most frequently was Masaccio's *Trinity* in the church of Santa Maria Novella in Florence. This is not to ignore the significance of his daily pilgrimages to the Carmelite church to visit the Brancacci Chapel; but in the *Trinity* certain architectural and spatial concepts, which Alberti was putting into words at this same time, must have seemed to Piero to be already stated so rigorously, with such profound implications of a monumental *gravitas,* that from then on they must have become dear to his heart, causing him at this early stage to question some of the teachings of Domenico, and even the slender structural framework Domenico himself was then planning for the *Carnesecchi Tabernacle.* If, then, it might be inferred that during his visits to Santa Maria Novella Piero looked also at the *Genesis* frescoes, painted a few years previously in the Chiostro Verde (Green Cloister) of the same church by Paolo Uccello, his attitude to these frescoes must have been one of open criticism, for he was surely conscious of the uncertainty and disorder of the world newly emerged from the flood, as it appeared to the mind of Uccello — a flood, of course, in the manner of Masaccio, even though Masaccio was mistakenly confused with the tender Ghiberti.

There is a belief, which dies hard, that Piero adhered to Uccello's arcane science of perspective.[4] This belief is contradicted not only by considerations of chronology, but by the fact that Piero himself chose as his master Domenico Veneziano rather than Uccello, and in consequence started his career in Sant'Egidio rather than San Miniato.[5] This is a choice which confirms Domenico Veneziano as a legitimate heir to Masaccio.[6] According to Longhi, Piero found in Masaccio's art the principle of a space enclosed and almost violated by the large scale of the figures; but quite apart from the two-dimensional dislocation of Brunelleschi's perspective, he must also have drawn from Masaccio the idea of a new relationship between figure and surroundings, a humanization of the scale of the architecture or landscape of the background which brings with it a naturalization of the figure: man as landscape.

The lesson of the Santa Maria Novella *Trinity* in this connection seems to me extremely clear: whether or not his 'great friend' Brunelleschi helped him in drawing out the perspective, Masaccio has here created for the first time in painting an architectonic, autonomous event, whose stylistic innovations were able to inspire Alberti, and Piero with him, with more than one fruitful line of thought. Besides, the problem goes far beyond one of style and becomes a matter of world-view (*Weltanschauung*): in both the Brancacci frescoes and Santa Maria Novella, Masaccio rejects the artificial formula of man as conqueror of nature, in favour of a concept of absolute natural dignity, of a total humanization of reality, so that there is made to correspond to the upright and unbending Apostles in the Brancacci Chapel a landscape of hills and houses equally rugged and unyielding, while the six monumental figures in the *Trinity* are seen against a stone monument of equal solemnity and power. This is not, of course, a question of ' scene-setting ': neither landscape nor architecture merely fulfils the function of providing a background to the action of the protagonists, for this background itself is charged with the same significance as the human beings. To confirm this, we need go no farther than the houses placed behind the scene of the *Resurrection of Tabitha* in the Brancacci Chapel: the short ' human ' episodes do not by themselves suffice to create the atmosphere of a heavy, sleepy afternoon, so much a part of everyday experience, as Longhi has pointed out.

It is at this point that the loss of the Sant'Egidio frescoes is so irreparable to our understanding of the continuity of the line which leads from Masaccio to Domenico Veneziano and Piero della Francesca. Domenico Veneziano most probably arrived in Florence while Masaccio was still alive, if, in the early 1430s, he painted the extraordinary *Adoration of the Magi* now in Berlin; and the walls of the church of Sant'Egidio surely provided the missing link in the chain from Masaccio to Filippo Lippi and later to Andrea del Castagno. We might have learnt from these frescoes what we cannot learn from the small number of his works that survive, namely why it was that Piero later turned in one direction while the Florentine artists who were influenced by Domenico Veneziano turned the other way — Alesso Baldovinetti, for example, and more especially Antonio Pollaiuolo who, treating the humanism of Masaccio in terms of the boundless energy of the cosmos, transformed perspective into space, and light into an accident of space, thus opening the way to the speculations of Leonardo.

In my view there seems no doubt that from these later developments, as well as from the achievements of the Magnoli altarpiece and sections of its predella, one may infer that Domenico Veneziano's frescoes in Sant'Egidio conveyed a subtle understanding of Masaccio's equation ' man = nature '; besides, in the Berlin tondo *Adoration of the Magi*, this idea forms the basis for an expression of a view of nature which was unique in its time.[7]

It is more difficult to go further than this definable mental affinity and say to what extent Domenico Veneziano was indebted to Masaccio for his view of mutation of colour by light. The problem is rendered almost insoluble, not only by the loss of the Sant'Egidio frescoes, but by the thick patina covering those in the Brancacci Chapel, although a glimmer of the original material (preserved almost intact by its covering of a later architectural structure, now removed) encourages the hope that one day it may at last be revealed through cleaning.

In my view, however, that ' light ' which was Domenico Veneziano's and later Piero's, was of the same substance as in Masaccio's pictorial vision. This may be seen by the way in which certain heads of apostles ' turn ' (St John in *St Peter's shadow healing the sick*) in the Brancacci Chapel, or in the brightness of the skin of St John's legs in the London *Baptism of Christ*, or again, and to an even greater extent, in the broad yet taut surfaces of the architectural motifs, which would make Landino's definition of ' pure... without ornamentation ' appear more apt by transferring it to an immediately visual plane (' pure ' being understood in the sense of ' clear and luminous '). Nor do I consider that a Masaccio who is ' clear ' (and this does not mean the abolition of chiaroscuro or a reduction of the dynamic vitality of the sculptural forms to a static volumetric representation) is incompatible with the idea of him which his contemporaries must have held.

If Masaccio and Domenico Veneziano were the two poles in Florence between which Piero gravitated, while meditating at the same time on Alberti's writings (his *Trattato della Pittura* had appeared a few years previously), it is probable that in Masaccio he looked for an existential meaning which was already changing, in Domenico Veneziano, into the ornamentation of narrative: the archaic element in Piero della Francesca may be attributed not so much to a mysterious and hidden affinity with the world-view of the Greeks and Romans as to the early humanists' exaggerated conception of the sublime in antiquity, which led to the ideal of *florentinitas* being identified with an ideal *romanitas* to signify a coincidence of values, both political (the liberty of the Roman citizen held up as an ideal by the citizens of Florence) and cultural (the history of the Ancients viewed as the history which nourishes the present: the basic idea of humanism).

The part played by artists in this current of thought which, while preaching a solemn adherence to the art of antiquity, began the modern era, is too well known to require emphasis here: what cannot be denied is that the sources of the substance of early Renaissance thought lie in the work of the first artists of the period, Brunelleschi, Donatello, Masaccio, Alberti, Nanni and Luca. It is this, rather than the formal elements in Piero's painting, that constitutes his direct debt to Masaccio. As we have seen, Domenico Veneziano had already turned the political implications of his masters into a more personal narrative, in line with the evolution of Florentine culture which was passing from a republican and popular order to the heraldic, courtly and even neo-Gothic ethos of the Medici.[8] Piero was probably concerned with the problem of transposing into a rustic setting the urban workpeople depicted by Masaccio, and he set out to express in his ' noble peasants ' the convictions substantiated by the movement of rebirth and revolt. In such an extension of the revolutionary idea from town to country there is even a parallel with the usual way popular movements develop, first in the urban proletariat and later in the agricultural community; there is no doubt that the only true heir of the politico-social humanism of the early fifteenth century triad is Piero himself, and this supports my conclusion that the Renaissance proper began in Florence and ended in the upper Tiber Valley, and that when it was outside these limits its nature changed into something of a different spirit which was more easily understood in a general European context.[9]

Piero's adherence to the fundamental spirit of humanism (and it may be imagined that his favourite ancient texts were certain parts of the *Odyssey, Aeneid* and *Georgics*

— Evander is certainly a character who can be understood in the spirit of Piero — and that his heroes were Cincinnatus and Fabius Maximus or even Cato) led him throughout his life to represent human beings as wise, bronzed figures, informed with a calm strength (at the same time as Sandro Botticelli was painting his neurotic, complex Madonnas). It is this adherence that probably accounts for the disdain with which the Florentines treated him after he left their city to return to Borgo. Once the spirit which had united the citizens of Florence during the early part of the century had withered away under Medici influence, Piero's language must have appeared archaic to them. He would have seemed to be surpassed at more than one point by the subtle innovations being prepared by artists of the second and third generation, while even his all-embracing love of nature would have appeared unequal to the pantheist spirit in which Pollaiuolo was to improve on the examples of Masaccio and Domenico Veneziano.[10] On the other hand, the good fortune Piero enjoyed at the courts (courts, not republican governments) of the Montefeltros in Urbino, the Malatestas in Rimini, the Este family in Ferrara, and the Pope in Rome, is to be explained by the fact that these potentates understood humanism in its cultural, not its political (Florentine) aspect, and could recognize in Piero an actual revival of antiquity, with all that *solemnitas* and *dignitas* of which Alberti speaks. [11]

If Piero's first work, the *Virgin and Child* in the Contini Bonacossi collection (ill. on p. 13) was painted while he was working closely with Domenico Veneziano, the London *Baptism of Christ* is obviously a Florentine work, both in origin and in precise references (*pls 1-2*): the landscape is that of Domenico's Berlin *Adoration of the Magi* brought to a higher degree of sureness and a more exact relationship with the figures. While Domenico was already following his natural inclination for fable, as a precursor to Pollaiuolo (in this same Berlin tondo one might try a photomontage with Hercules and Deianeira in place of the Magi and their procession), Piero re-stated Masaccio's equation of 'man = nature', and any change he introduced into Masaccio's conception was in the direction of channelling both will

Virgin and Child (see p. 30)

and energy into a sort of calm ritualistic strength. A hint of the direction Piero was shortly to take appears already in the relationship between the extremely white tree trunk and the figures standing around it; they are all presented with equal dignity in an integrated conception of man and nature, where one and the same spirit breathes through the landscape and through man. We can see how from the very first Piero felt a sympathy for the solemn ritual of rural life, where the rhythms of labour in the fields are the same as in the days of Hesiod and Homer.[12]

The synthesis was now complete: just as Brunelleschi's perspective had enabled Masaccio to emphasize the humanity of his Apostles, so too in his spacious and luminous representation of nature Piero found the setting for the dignified movements of his calm heroes.[13]

The same observation may be made in connection with the other work of Piero's which was at least partially of the same period, the *Polyptych of the Misericordia*, in Borgo San Sepolcro, commissioned on 11 January 1445 with the stipulation that it was to be completed by 1448, but probably not completed before 1458, as can be seen from the stylistic disparity among the different panels (ills on pp. 15 and 31, *pls 3-7*). The part of the polyptych which appears to be the earliest, painted at the same time as the *Baptism of Christ*, is the section on the left representing St Sebastian and St John the Baptist (*pls 4-5*). Without dwelling on the similarity between these figures and those of Masaccio, one cannot fail to notice the relationship between man and nature achieved in spite of the absence of a landscape background (the donors had insisted on a gold ground). This seems paradoxical, but is not so, for Piero based his dialogue on the ' human ' quality of the picture, of which he made an architectonic landscape such as he could have developed out of Masaccio's *Trinity*. This gave rise to Longhi's brilliant comment: ' In the architectonic partition of the polyptych into perfect hundredths, the saints are arranged as if under the arch of a sun-drenched Albertian portico, and they themselves become a temple and a measure of the temple, in the original sense in which the spatial " templum " was established and circumscribed by the ancient augur; since on looking more closely at the two-dimensional representation of the figures, one finds that they include space within them, and are in fact constructed in a measured depth.'[14]

This observation seems to me equally apt to the two first saints, although Longhi sees in them a predominance of

Polyptych of the Misericordia: St Andrew and St Bernardine (see *p. 31)*

15

sculpture over measure, ' as in Masaccio '. ' Measure ' itself
is an essential aspect of the actual partition and invention
of the polyptych, and must therefore be considered part of
the initial inspiration of the artist, and not something which
occurred to him later as an afterthought, even though in
the saints on the right, in the small top panels and in the
central section, the relation between image and architecture
appears more fully thought out and carefully weighed. [15]
The sense of a solemn ritual which has been referred to
is again present here, not in the form of action, since the
characters are presented in a state of immobile contempla-
tion, but in the classical ideal of nobility which they embody.
They are shown as absorbed participants in a sacred event
or, more precisely, as members of a procession grouped
around the standard of the Virgin (an idol worn smooth by
the reverent worship of the faithful), which passes through
the countryside to exorcise drought and bring a promise
of hope for the next rains. The sense of the holiness of the
essential acts of life remained a constant element in Piero's
view of humanity; from this his poetic world sprang.
The two dated works Piero is known to have painted in
addition to the *Polyptych of the Misericordia* and before
he began work on the Arezzo frescoes (probably in 1445,
soon after the death of Bicci di Lorenzo, who had originally
been entrusted with the decoration) are the Berlin *St Jerome* and the fresco, *St Sigismund honoured by Sigismondo
Malatesta*, in the Tempio Malatestiano in Rimini, both
signed PETRI DE BURGO OPUS, the former dated MCCCL,
and the latter MCCCCLI.
Previous works included the Venice *St Jerome with a
penitent* (*pl. 8*), believed by Longhi to be of the same period as the London *Baptism of Christ* and the first part of
the *Polyptych of the Misericordia*, and the Urbino *Flagellation* (*pls 9-11*), while the profile *Portrait of Sigismondo
Malatesta* in the Contini Bonacossi collection is ' certainly
of 1451 because it is so closely related to the portrait of
Malatesta in the Rimini fresco, even to its size ' (Longhi:
see also p. 32).
In *St Jerome with a penitent*, the natural indications
already present in the *Baptism of Christ* and other early

16

Florentine works of Piero are seen more and more in terms of landscape, so that St Jerome in the desert and his devout companion are as much a part of space in landscape as are the mountains or the distant city, and there is no longer any need to place the tree in the centre of the scene, as in the *Baptism of Christ*, in order to proclaim the man-nature relationship, now created by the all-pervading glow of the atmosphere in which the action becomes one with the essential immobility of nature.

In the *Flagellation* (*pls 9-11*), if the figure of the youth on the right represents Oddantonio da Montefeltro between the two evil counsellors, Manfredo Pio and Tommaso dell'Agnello, then this painting must have been produced after 1444, the year of the death of Montefeltro. I agree with Longhi [16] that it could not have been painted much later than this date, for although it is close to Alberti in its architectonic and spatial structure, it has a geometric exactness, a feeling for architecture as a spatial background to man (even if the relationship is one of equality), which must have been a current topic of discussion in Florentine circles at the time Piero might have frequented them. In the Rimini fresco, the architecture provides a sense of ritual, while in the Arezzo series it has an air of deliberateness and is intended to give a framework which seems to be the outdoor counterpart to Masaccio's *Trinity*, and certain parts of the work — the small palace on the right and the well-defined iron brackets — are faintly reminiscent of the houses in the Brancacci Chapel.

Until now Piero had been building up landscape in an architectonic form in which the human figure was treated as another column, providing a framework for the painting. In the *Flagellation* the problem becomes one of a relationship of architecture as architecture (instead of architecture as landscape) with man, and was therefore in harmony with Piero's early ideas. From this point of view it is not certain whether this painting may not have been an earlier work than the Venice *St Jerome with a penitent* (which, as we have seen, was already a natural unity in which architecture and landscape were equally absorbed) but in any case the two works cannot have been far apart.

In the *Flagellation* men and columns, architraves, ceilings and paving stones are equally involved in the action, of which space is an essential element. Masaccio's *Trinity* is recollected in the superbly integrated framework; the action partakes of the inevitability of a natural episode, and the human landscape has now become landscape pure and simple.

As for the painting *St Jerome in penitence* in the Berlin Staatliche Museen, it is now impossible to place it within Piero's trend of ideas because a considerable amount of it was painted by other hands; only the foreground was by Piero, and as compared with the background in the manner of a marriage chest, it shows superb mastery (see p. 32).

The works of Piero so far catalogued include, besides those produced when he was first at Borgo San Sepolcro (the *Baptism of Christ* painted for the Prioria di San Giovanni, and the *Polyptych of the Misericordia* painted for the Brotherhood of Mercy), work done for the court of Urbino (*Flagellation*) and for the Castello Estense in Ferrara (frescoes, now lost, commissioned about 1449). The parallel course followed by the journeys of Piero and Alberti is now well known, as is Piero's influence on the course of fifteenth-century art: the importance of Alberti's *Veglie Urbinate* in the development of the art of the provinces and in the formation of a culture in which lie the origins of Raphael and Bramante is now an accepted fact; so too is the effect of his journey to Ferrara, as well as his later travels in the Romagna and Marches, on the art of the northern part of Italy. One need only perhaps insist on Alberti's transposition of Florentine humanism into terms of refinement and nobility, and on his constant emphasis on a rock-like solidity which in his turn Piero introduced into these concepts

The journey to Rimini set the seal on Piero's friendship with Alberti. There is still doubt as to how far Alberti may be considered indebted to Piero for the ' colour ' which imbued his architecture of the Tempio Malatestiano, but I feel certain that both artists continually returned in spirit to the example of Masaccio's *Trinity*, where the architecture, even to its sense of colour, is exactly as Alberti was later to conceive it. The same may be said also of Piero's fresco,

St Sigismund honoured by Sigismondo Malatesta (*pls 12-15*).
Here it seems very likely that there is more than one
direct reminiscence of certain of Masaccio's works, for
example, the small *Adoration of the Magi*, now in Berlin,
where the section on the right showing two horses reversed
in colour and position appears as a necessary precedent to
Piero's subtle epigram of the two greyhounds accompanying
Sigismondo.

We have now come to the years of Arezzo. In the choir of
San Francesco Piero finally found the largeness of scale
he needed in order to expand and test his skill to its limit.
The sky of Arezzo in the background is the final great
episode of the tradition created by Giotto at Assisi: a
civilization narrating its own history among the halls through
which it moves day by day. Meanwhile, Mantegna at Man-
tua, Cossa and Roberti in Ferrara, to mention only the
greatest, illustrated the palaces of noblemen with sacred
and profane allegories and myths, while in Florence after
Domenico Veneziano Benozzo Gozzoli transformed the
thorny subject of the Council into an ingenuous festive pag-
eantry; later Ghirlandaio was to reduce the same subject
to the level of reportage. To find the reality of history, in
both spirit and fact, we must turn to the matchless annals
of Giotto, of Masaccio, of Piero and the other artists
whose works reconstruct the history of town and country,
of active men conscious of their humanity and their acts.
I do not include Michelangelo; profoundly convinced of
his own superhuman mission, he transcended this historical
and national consciousness.

Once the frescoes at Arezzo have been seen, even Piero's
earliest works, the *Baptism of Christ* and the *Flagellation*,
acquire greater depth: not that it is a good thing to write
history in reverse, but certain of the ideas already present in
these early works are stated conclusively as part of Piero's
broad grasp of narrative. As for the theme, it exists only as a
subject personal to Piero: the courts of men of past times,
lands where the eternal ritual of life moves with a calm,
immemorial certitude. The slender thread of history in
the story of the Cross disappears in these isolated episodes,
and we look at the frescoes without being aware of any

external reference. If, in Masaccio, there is complete identity between historical pretext and representation, and the deeds of the apostles are situated firmly in present-day reality, this is because these deeds are historically effective, in the sense that their value is enduring; through a similar conviction of the 'morality' of art, Piero removed his painting from the realm of fable and staked all his cards on the simple truth of the scenes he presented. It was only in the scenes involving Adam (*pls 18-20*) that he was able to fit legend into his history, since no other scene had appeared to him so prophetic, so intimately linked to an understanding of the present, as this planting of the root of humanity.

For the rest, the scenes are straightforward and solemn: the *Queen of Sheba visits Solomon* (*pls 21-5*) is a meeting of royal personages; the *Removal of the Sacred Bridge* (*pl. 26*) is a rustic scene; the *Dream of Constantine* (*pls 30-1*) carries a feeling of a deep and heavy sleep after much fatigue; the *Victory of Constantine over Maxentius* and the *Victory of Heraclius over Chosroes* (*pls 32-5, 46-9*) are two battle scenes where fifteenth-century historical painting once again becomes imbued with the spirit of Virgil; the *Torture of the Jew Judas* (*pls 36-7*), which if not actually a historical event, represents a moment of life; the *Finding and proof of the Cross* (*pls 38-45*) and *Heraclius brings back the Cross to Jerusalem* (*pls 50-4*) are two great rites in a simple and ancient cult, such as befitted the descendants of the dying Adam, charged with all the years of humanity. And in this coherent cycle of action and existence, we must not overlook the fact that the only sign of divine intervention is an announcement, not of birth, but of death (*Annunciation of the Death of the Virgin, pls 27-9*),[17] a necessary and supreme episode in the cycle of life.

In these frescoes the moment of existence is arrested so completely that the human and historical significance of the action seems in itself to comprise an essential immobility, as if, having reached the limit of narrative possibilities, Piero had stabilized his action at a supreme level. No later development in his style would seem to change the essential stability he had now reached, although such developments did make themselves apparent in a greater harmony of colour and volume and greater breadth of design from the time of the Monterchi *Madonna in Pregnancy* (*pls 16-17*), which is the immediate predecessor of the Arezzo frescoes, until the final episodes of the fresco cycle in San Francesco, the *Victory of Heraclius over Chosroes,* and the *St Mary Magdalene* in Arezzo Cathedral (*pl. 55*), similar to the Virgin of the *Annunciation* in the way the body turns slightly. This impression is reinforced by the easel paintings which were produced at the same time as the Arezzo frescoes: the Borgo *Resurrection of Christ* (*pls 56-7*), *St Julian*, also in Borgo (see p. 36), the Boston *Hercules* and the Lehman *St Apollonia* (see p. 36), are all impregnated with the same ' non-eloquence ', an extremely simplified language and style in which emphasis is placed on the element of ritual and the iconographic value of the image.

The *Resurrection of Christ* deserves separate treatment. The this-worldly (and profoundly humanistic) treatment of some of the figures in the *Finding and proof of the Cross* and *Heraclius brings back the Cross to Jerusalem* is here repeated with such intensity that we can recognize in the figure of Christ that same figure that Masaccio had painted crucified and dead (in the *Trinity* in Santa Maria Novella and in the *Crucifixion* in the Pisan polyptych), now finally risen. This provides a symbolic conclusion to the parabola of humanism. The fact that the dawn upon which Christ looks is the sure path from the rational clarity of Masaccio to the luminous landscapes of Antonello and Giovanni Bellini is a further proof of the extraordinarily far-reaching effects of the early thought of the century, out of which modern painting was born.

After Arezzo, little seems to have changed in Piero's work during the ten years from 1460-70, when he painted the Augustinian and Perugian polyptychs and the diptych of the Montefeltros, yet one can see in these works that against the volumetric framework of the images there is taking root a subtle, barely visible violation of anatomy, while the landscapes are disturbed by an element of disquiet, more pervasive and animistic than in previous works. This may be thought an exaggeration of the impression given by Piero's work at that stage, but we shall see on considering his later paintings how this decade marked a considerable development from the style of his Arezzo period.

The terms 'anatomy' and 'an animistic view of nature' are essential points of reference in dealing with the culture of Florence during those years; this is revealed above all in the work of Antonio Pollaiuolo, who by about the year 1457 had already produced *St Mary the Egyptian*, now in Staggia, near Siena; in 1466 he was working on the first designs for embroideries for *St John's Vestment*, and on the extraordinary *Tobias and the Angel* in Turin. Still more important was the commission given him in 1460 to paint the three large canvases on the subject of *The Labours of Hercules* for the Medici palace. Pollaiuolo's path diverged from Piero's, for throughout the whole period of the work at Arezzo Piero was largely concerned with the architectonic expression of the man-nature equation which originated in Masaccio.

There is no reason to doubt that Piero visited Florence during this period (and in fact it is very likely that he had been there a few times during his long stay in Arezzo), and the extent of his contact with Pollaiuolo may be inferred from the paintings he executed at the time. Given the indisputable fact of the prior dating of Pollaiuolo's Florentine works, Piero's later works show the influence of Florentine taste, and actually provide the solution to the problems which were then plaguing poor Signorelli, in his desperate attempt to find a middle way between the immobility of Piero and the movement of Pollaiuolo in painting, whereby the motionless figures taken from Arezzo assume the gestures of Pollaiuolo's crossbowmen.

In the works produced during the 1460s, as we have seen, there is hardly a trace of suspicion that such a development was taking place. It first became apparent in Piero's *Diptych of the Dukes of Montefeltro* (*pls 67-70*), where landscape is shown in a bird's eye view for the first time, and freed from the close constriction of an architectonic framework, just as it must have spread out behind Hercules in the lost *Labours of Hercules* canvases by Pollaiuolo. Some idea of what these paintings may have been like can be gathered from the two small panels on a similar subject in the Uffizi. It is clear, however, that Piero still held to the constructive function of the image which formed an architectonic foreground to the landscape — the very same conception as had run through all his work from as far back as the London *Baptism of Christ*.

With reference to his emphasis on anatomy, this is to be understood in the volumetric rigour of the image, an initial attempt at making the figures participate in the animistic landscape without detracting from their monumentality: this is an equilibrium most difficult to attain, but superbly realized in Piero's *Nativity*, in London (*pls 75-6*), a work which might have been painted by a non-Florentine (and greater) Pollaiuolo, and perhaps Piero's masterpiece. But already certain attitudes of the hands in the two polyptychs (*pls 58-60*, ill. on p. 37, *pls 61-6*), and certain anatomical features of the draperies in the Perugia *Baptism* and *St John the Evangelist* in the Frick Collection (ill. on p. 25), speak clearly and lead us to seek for some typically Florentine current in the later works. But before passing to these, this is perhaps the moment to consider the fact that at about this same time in the cope worn by the figure of St Augustine in the *St Augustine Polyptych* (*pl. 58*), Piero undertook a task similar to Pollaiuolo's *Vestment of St John*, resolving through paint that which Pollaiuolo had entrusted to his embroiderers, although we should not perhaps go so far as to think of this as an imitation of Pollaiuolo or rivalry with the Florentine artist.

But to go further, the Williamstown *Virgin and Child with angels* (*pls 71-2*) is perhaps the closest precedent to the *Brera Altarpiece*, not only for its calculated arrangement of space, but for its anatomical perception, noticeable particularly in the clothes of the two angels at the sides, who are quite closely related to Piero Pollaiuolo's *Virtues* in the Mercatanzia (1469-70). Much greater in achievement is without doubt the *Sinigallia Madonna* (*pls 73-4*), in which the anatomy suggested by the drapery is resolved in volume and colour and the monumental and the intimate meet, as Longhi has noted, in the wall in the background where Piero's usual restrained architecture becomes less rigid and more a part of everyday life; the Virgin, who is descended from the ladies of the Queen of Sheba, while losing nothing of the usual ritual solemnity, has become more alive and approachable. This was a most important turning-point in Piero's art, since it testified to his evolution, after the example of Florence, from intellectualism to a more subjective and individual attitude which immediately preludes the London *Nativity*. In this work, as we have seen, the sacred event becomes merged in a cosmic awareness of nature which penetrates the figures, bathed in an entirely new vibrant colour and in a broad atmospheric treatment anticipating Leonardo (*pls 75-6*).

We now come to the *Brera Altarpiece* (*pls 77-80*), which stands in a relationship to the London *Nativity* similar to that which has been observed between the *Baptism of Christ* and the *Flagellation*, shifting the emphasis between the problem of the new harmony between man and natural ' architecture ' (resolved in ' nature ' pure and simple) and the other harmony between man and architecture. If man is still a structural element in the picture of an ornate society, Piero captures at the same time the vibration of the sun's rays which give substance to colour, through the movement of an anatomy which is in itself vibrant, pre-Leonardesque. It was no chance that in this development there reappeared the original great inspiration of Masaccio's *Trinity*, thus completing the first and greatest period of the Tuscan and Italian Renaissance.

Piero and the Critics

For a complete account of critical attitudes to Piero della Francesca, see the previously mentioned monograph by Longhi, first published in 1927 and republished in 1942. The third edition, published by Sansoni in Longhi's *Opera Omnia* (Florence 1961 etc.), covers the additional period 1927-63. His essay *Piero in Arezzo* appeared, revised and corrected, in Switzerland in 1950 and later in *Paragone*. It

St Augustine Polyptych: St Michael and St John the Evangelist (see p. 37)

should be added that the notes to the text and illustrations have been updated to take account of the latest criticism, much of which is the work of Longhi himself. Longhi's work forms the basis for all criticism of Piero della Francesca, and it is to this work, as well as to his basic study ' Piero dei Franceschi e lo sviluppo della pittura veneziana ' (written in 1913 and published in 1914 in *L'Arte*, and republished in the *Opera Omnia*, I) that the contemporary esteem in which the painter is held is to a large extent to be ascribed, both from the strictly scientific point of view and, more generally, from the point of view of appreciation.

I give below a list of works which form an essential bibliography on Piero della Francesca, in addition to the two texts by Piero himself, *De Prospectiva pingendi*, published in a critical edition by Giusta Nicco Fasola (Florence 1942), and *De quinque corporibus regolaribus*, which was published by Luca Pacioli as his own work a few years after Piero's death.

J. von Schlossier, ' Piero della Francesca ', *Sitzungsberichte der Wiener Akademie*, Vienna 1929-33; U. Gnoli, 'Una tavola sconosciuta di Piero della Francesca ', *Dedalo*, 1930; A. Stokes, *The Quattrocento. A different Conception of the Italian Renaissance*, I, London 1932; R. Longhi, *Officina Ferrarese*, Rome, 1934 (2nd ed. Florence 1956); M. Salmi, ' Paolo Uccello, Domenico Veneziano, Piero della Francesca e gli affreschi del Duomo di Prato ', *Bollettino d'Arte*, 1934; P. Toesca, ' Piero della Francesca ', *Enciclopedia Italiana*, XVII, 1935, pp. 208-13; A. Chastel, ' La légende de la Reine de Saba ', *Revue d'Histoire des Religions*, 1939; M. Salmi, *Gli affreschi di San Francesco in Arezzo*, Bergamo 1940; R. Longhi, ' Fatti di Masolino e di Masaccio ', *La Critica d'Arte,* Florence 1940; R. Longhi, ' Genio degli anonimi. I, Giovanni di Piemonte ', *La Critica d'Arte*, 1940; M. Meiss, ' A Documented Altarpiece by Piero della Francesca ', *The Art Bulletin*, 1941; J. Lauts, ' Zu Piero della Francescas verlorene Fresken in Ferrara ', *Zeitschrift für Kunstgeschichte*, 1941-2; F. Arcangeli, *Tarsie*, Rome 1942; G. Nicco Fasola, ' Lo svolgimento del pensiero prospettico nei trattati da Euclide a Piero della Francesca ', *Le Arti*, 1942; M. Salmi, ' Piero della Francesca e Giuliano Amedei ', *Rivista d'Arte*, 1942; M. Salmi, ' La Bibbia di Borso d'Este e Piero della Francesca ', *La Rinascita*, 1943; M. Salmi, *Piero della Francesca e il Palazzo Ducale di Urbino*, Florence 1945; M. Salmi, ' Un'ipotesi su Piero della Francesca ', *Arti figurative*, 1947; Kenneth Clark, ' Piero della Francesca's St Augustine Altarpiece ', *The Burlington Magazine*, 1947; Kenneth Clark, *Landscape into Art*, London

1949; A. Stokes, *Art and Science*, London 1949; A. Chastel, 'La Rencontre de Salomon et de la Reine de Saba dans l'iconographie médiévale', *Gazette des Beaux-Arts*, 1949; R. Longhi, ' Piero in Arezzo ', *Paragone*, 1950; B. Berenson, *Piero della Francesca o dell'arte non eloquente*, Florence 1950; P. Rotondi, *Il Palazzo Ducale di Urbino*, Urbino 1950-1; Kenneth Clark, *Piero della Francesca*, London 1951; R. Longhi, ' Il Maestro di Pratovecchio ', *Paragone*, 35, 1952; F. Wittgens, *La pala urbinate di Piero,* Milan 1952; *Catalogo della Mostra dei Quattro Maestri in Palazzo Strozzi* (the section on Piero edited by L. Berti), Florence 1954; J. Pope Hennessy, *Piero della Francesca*, New York 1954; M. Meiss, ' Ovum Struthionis, Symbol and Allusion in Piero della Francesca's Montefeltro Altarpiece ', *Studies in Art Literature for Belle da Costa Green,* Princeton University Press 1954; M. Meiss, ' Addendum Ovologicum ', *The Art Bulletin*, 1954; M. Salmi (on the Saint by Piero della Francesca uncovered in San Sepolcro on 23 December 1954), in *Bollettino d'Arte*, 1955; D. Formaggio, *Piero della Francesca*, Milan 1957; F. Zeri, *Due dipinti, la filologia e un nome,* Turin 1961; A. Parronchi, ' Paolo o Piero? ', *Studi di Storia dell'arte per R. Longhi, Arte Antica e Moderna*, 1961; S. Bottari, article on ' Piero della Francesca ', *Enciclopedia of World Art*, London 1963; M. Salmi, ' Le storie della Croce ', *Forma e Colore*, 14, 1966. For writings on Urbino see A. Chastel, *The Golden Age of the Renaissance*, and *Studios and Styles of the Renaissance,* London and New York 1966.

Notes on the Text

[1] This definition signifies more than the usual laudatory epithets: if the message of Florentine humanism was carried through the Italian provinces (which were to become artistic capitals) this was largely owing to Piero and to the journeys of Donatello and Andrea del Castagno to Venice and of Fra Angelico and Domenico Veneziano in Umbria. Then, of course, there was Alberti, whose travels, significantly, nearly always ran parallel to Piero's.

[2] G. Milanesi, ' Le vite di alcuni artefici fiorentini scritte da G. Vasari... Vita di Piero della Francesca ', *Giornale storico degli Artisti toscani*, VI, 1862.

[3] According to A. Venturi and Longhi, and I think one must agree, this ' panel ', of which we have no other record, is of that *Eucharist* whose predella had been painted by Piero. It was later entrusted to Justus of Ghent, in 1474, since Piero had apparently been unable to come to an agreement with the donors.

[4] At the time when Piero was in Florence, about 1439, he was not yet fully formed as an artist. ' In those still curiously prehistoric times [1927, first edition of Longhi's monograph on Piero], it had not yet become clear from documentary evidence, although such evidence was already in existence, how very much more slowly Paolo Uccello developed; and now his importance to the art of Piero seems to me almost insignificant. ' (R. Longhi, *Piero della Francesca*, additional notes to the second edition [1942], *Opera Omnia*, III, Florence 1963, p. 195.)

[5] It would be very interesting to imagine the conversations that might have taken place between Piero, as an apprentice in San Miniato, and Paolo Uccello: we would probably see in them a parallel to the dialogues which took place fifteen years earlier between Masaccio and Masolino in the Carmine.

[6] A hypothesis which Luciano Berti has refuted with his usual subtlety: ' A counter-argument — as seductive as all novelties and contradictions — would tend... to make us feel dismay before a Masaccio who had disappeared without an heir; to discount the variety of points at which his influence was felt as being unable to reproduce faithfully the full message of Masaccio; and finally to consider as the exception to the rule a non-Florentine, Domenico Veneziano, and his follower Piero della Francesca ' (L. Berti, *Andrea del Castagno*, Florence 1966).

[7] For the most penetrating analysis of Domenico Veneziano's position in the context of Florentine culture, see the basic study by Longhi, ' Il Maestro di Pratovecchio ', *Paragone*, 35, 1962.

[8] It is no accident that Cosimo de' Medici preferred the ' Gothic ' Michelozzo to the revolutionary Brunelleschi, since he was probably not unaware of the symbolic value assumed, for example, by the cupola of the Cathedral of Florence, so completely understood by Alberti (' so as to cover with its shade all the Tuscan peoples ').

See by the present writer, *Botticelli*, in the present series (1968), and ' Introduzione al Rinascimento ' in *Umanesimo e Rinascimento, (Il Mondo delle Forme, VI)*, Florence 1966.

[9] A ' proletarian ' interpretation of the early Renaissance will possibly conflict with the refined humanism of politicians and men of letters (for example, Coluccio Salutati and Leonardo Bruni), but is in my opinion justified in the figurative arts, which by their nature and intention are, or were, far more popular than *humanae litterae*.

[10] I have made an attempt to construct a hypothetical argument between Pollaiuolo and Piero on the subject of the heritage of Masaccio (' Antonio Pollaiolo: il parlamento di S. Giovanni ', *Forma e Colore*, 24, 1966). Masaccio's two most authentic — and opposed — heirs were in fact Piero della Francesca and Antonio Pollaiuolo (and following the latter, Leonardo), since they had most fully understood Masaccio's conception of nature. At least in part, the roots of Michelangelo were different (Botticelli was the determining influence in his case), although he is sometimes referred to, rather sweepingly, as a continuation of the parabola Giotto-Masaccio.

[11] In this brief recapitulation of the origins of Piero, the ' Sienese question' has not been touched upon, but it has been explained fully by Longhi in the study referred to above on the Master of Pratovecchio. A young man of Piero's temperament must have been so overwhelmed by the wealth of invention and experiment taking place while he was in Florence that there could have been no room for any other kind of influence. Moreover, as Longhi has shown, the spiral of the Sienese Renaissance, from Domenico di Bartolo to Sassetta, has its roots in the work of Domenico Veneziano. Nor does the idea seem acceptable that Piero in Florence could have taken as a fundamental theme for his imagery the memory of the Tiber landscape at the time of his stay in Florence, for it was only after his study of Masaccio's frescoes that he was able to appreciate its spatial quality.

[12] Alfredo Panzini has noted that in Romagna ' the beautiful Latin word survives, I know not how, and we still call the tools of labour *armi, arma armorum* '. And to Piero, far more than to us in our industrial era, agriculture must have seemed an essentially noble occupation, expressing immediately through its movements the resounding rhythm of a Greek hexameter.

[13] A ' formal ' view of Piero's work has already been presented in a masterly way by Longhi, and therefore I will not even attempt to state it briefly here. The whole of this present study can be no more than a marginal note to Longhi's great work.

[14] Longhi, *op. cit.*, p. 20.

[15] I think this dissimilarity is much more relevant to the work of Masaccio, which to my way of thinking was already consciously ' spatial ', than to Piero's, and the *Polyptych of the Misericordia* speaks with a single voice, in spite of an unevenness of style.

[16] In the third edition. of his monograph (p. 201) Longhi says he is inclined to date the Urbino painting a few years later.

Notes on Piero's Works

Virgin and Child. (Illustration in black and white on page 13.) On panel. Florence, Contini Bonacossi collection. On the back there is a perspective study of a vase, and beside it an inscription: 'By M. Lionardo da Vinco [*sic*]. Retouched by Sandro Rosi 1655'. Once the retouching had been removed, the *Virgin and Child* was found to have a very worn surface, in which the sharpness of outline has become rather blurred. Believed by Longhi to be Piero's earliest known work, it was painted in Florence while he was still in contact with Domenico Veneziano, that is, while he was working on the choir of Sant'Egidio. The drawing on the back is typical of Piero's preoccupation with the problems of perspective during those years (Longhi) and in line with the extraordinary drawing in the Uffizi (No. 1758 A) of a faceted vase, formely attributed to Paolo Uccello but justly included in the catalogue of Piero's work by Alessandro Parronchi (in ' Paolo o Piero? ', *Studi di Storia dell'Arte per R. Longhi, Arte Antica e Moderna*, 1961). It is curious to note that the seventeenth-century attribution of the painting to Leonardo, considering it an entirely Florentine work, draws the logical conclusions from a stylistic manner close to Domenico Veneziano, of whom Leonardo is the heir, though by way of Antonio Pollaiuolo.

1-2 Baptism of Christ. On panel. London, National Gallery. This work was painted for the Prioria di San Giovanni Battista in Borgo San Sepolcro, removed to the cathedral in 1807, and sold in 1857, eventually passing to the National Gallery. It is universally ascribed to Piero's first period, and is of the same style as the earliest part of the *Polyptych of the Misericordia*, that is, not later than 1445.

3-7 Polyptych of the Misericordia. (See also illustrations in black and white on pp. 15 and 31.) On panel. Museo di Borgo San Sepolcro. This is Piero's first documented work, commissioned by the Brotherhood of Mercy of Borgo San Sepolcro under a contract drawn up by Ser Mario Fedeli dal Borgo, stipulating that the work was to be completed by the end of 1448, at a price of 150 gold florins. Piero's hand can be recognized in the four *Saints* on the sides, in the *Virgin* in the centre, the two *Saints* and *Annunciation* in the second row, and in the *Crucifixion* which crowns the altarpiece. The predella and *Saints* on the pilasters are obviously the work of another hand, despite the clause in the contract under which the whole work was to be by Piero himself. The stylistic disparities within the polyptych indicate that its execution was spread over a long period of time; it was not completed until much later than the time specified, probably about the year 1462, when the Brotherhood paid to Marco di Benedetto ' fifteen crowns in part payment for the altarpiece which M. Piero his brother has painted '.

Schematic reconstruction of the Polyptych of the Misericordia

The chronological order of the individual panels may, I believe, be traced from the *St Sebastian* (*pl. 4*) and *St John the Baptist* (*pl. 5*) on the left, to the *Crucifixion* above (*pls 6-7*), the central *Virgin and Child* (*pl. 3*), *St Andrew* and *St Bernardin* on the right (ill. on p. 15), and finally the four small sections in the second row (*St Benedict, Angel, Virgin of the Annunciation, St Francis*), where the early monumental treatment of the figures, inspired by Masaccio, progressively yields to an emphasis on the atmospheric harmony of colour.

8 St Jerome with a penitent. On panel. Venice, Accademia. Below the figure of the penitent is the inscription: HIER. AMADI. AUG. F., indicating the Venetian origin of the donor (another Amadi, also a Venetian, commissioned paintings from Niccolò di Pietro and Gentile da Fabriano in 1408, as Cavalcaselle has pointed out). According

31

to Longhi (*Opera Omnia*, III, 1963), this might indicate a possible journey by Piero to Venice around 1450, when he was known to be at Ferrara, on the route to Venice. I myself believe that this assumption would place the painting at too late a date for its style, which is close to, and only slightly later than, that of the London *Baptism of Christ* and the first phase of the *Polyptych of the Misericordia.*

9-11 Flagellation. On panel. Urbino, Galleria Nazionale delle Marche. This painting is traditionally associated with the Serafini conspiracy, when Oddantonio da Montefeltro was assassinated (1444). He is thought to be represented in the fair-headed young man on the right flanked by his evil counsellors Manfredo Pio and Tommaso dell'Agnello. Again, by its stylistic features this work could not have been painted later than 1450, although there are many art historians who believe it to be contemporary with the Arezzo frescoes.

St Jerome in penitence. On panel. Berlin, Staatliche Museen. Signed and dated PETRI DE BURGO OPUS MCCCCL. It was bought for Berlin by Bode and catalogued by him in 1924. Only the figure of the saint, the seat and books and cupboard cut into the rock are the work of Piero. The remainder, though based on an original plan of his, is by a quite mediocre painter of the late fifteenth century.

12-15 St Sigismund honoured by Sigismondo Malatesta. Fresco. Rimini, Tempio Malatestiano, Reliquary Chapel. Signed and dated PETRI DE BURGO OPUS MCCCCLI. In a medallion on the right is the Malatesta Castle with the inscription CASTELLUM SISMUNDUM ARIMINENSE MCCCCXLVI, the year in which the Castle was built.

Portrait of Sigismondo Malatesta. On panel. Florence, Contini Bonacossi Collection. Brought into the corpus of Piero's works by Longhi in the second edition of his monograph. It must have been painted very near in time to the Rimini fresco, for which it probably served as a model.

16-17 Madonna in pregnancy. Fresco. Monterchi, Cemetery Chapel. This fresco most probably belongs to Piero's first Arezzo period, soon after his return from Rimini. It is to be hoped that the chapel will soon be restored to its original appearance after the havoc caused by successive restorations. Piero's fresco, with its extraordinary spatial recession, fulfilled the function of an illusory apse in the chapel.

Legend of the True Cross. Frescoes. Arezzo, Choir of the Church of San Francesco. See *pls 18-54.*

The decoration of the choir of San Francesco was begun in 1447 by Bicci di Lorenzo and interrupted by his death in 1452. Piero probably began work on it immediately afterwards and completed it before his journey to Rome in 1459. Bicci di Lorenzo was responsible for the frescoes on the ceiling and archway (except for the *Doctors of the Church Ambrose and Augustine,* by Piero); all the remainder was the work of Piero, apart from the two versions of *Christ with the symbols of the Passion* on the pillars in the entrance porch and *St Louis* and the *Blindfold Cupid* on the left pilaster, done by assistants. With regard to the chronological sequence of the episodes, the simplest and at the same time most likely solution to this by no means easy problem is that Piero painted all the right-hand wall first, obviously working from top to bottom, with the *Story of Adam, The Queen of Sheba visits Solomon* and the *Victory of Constantine over Maxentius*; he then painted the back wall, starting from the right side (a *Prophet, Removal of the Sacred Bridge, Dream of Constantine*), next those on the left side (a *Prophet, Torture of Judas, Annunciation of the Death of the Virgin*) and finally the frescoes on the left wall, *Heraclius Bringing the Cross to Jerusalem, Finding and proof of the Cross,* and the *Victory of Heraclius over Chosroes.* The likelihood that this is the correct order is strengthened by the fact that this order shows the progressive intervention of assistants: they are entirely absent from the paintings on the right-hand wall, but appear on the right side of the back in the *Removal of the Sacred Bridge,* on the left in the *Prophet* and the *Torture of the Jew Judas,* and in all the scenes on the left wall – to the greatest extent in the last episode, the *Victory of Heraclius over Chosroes.* The frescoes were recently restored by Leonetto Tintori with his usual skill and intelligence, and the original frescoes freed from successive layers of overpainting. It is to be hoped that the vast amount of relevant documentation will soon be published, so putting an end to the adverse criticism which has been voiced and for which there is little reason.

A detailed description of the frescoes now follows.

Two prophets. On the top right and left sides of the back wall. Iconography uncertain.

18-20   Death and burial of Adam. Lunette on the right-hand wall. This is certainly the first, both in subject order and in order of execution, as can be seen by the dry handling of the paint, which lacks the 'atmospheric' freedom of the frescoes of the second and first row. On the right is the figure of the dying Adam, ordering his son Seth to ask the guardian angel of the Earthly Paradise for the oil of salvation promised to him at the time of the Expulsion (*pl. 20*). Instead Seth obtained from the angel three seeds which were to be placed in his father's mouth. On the left, Seth is shown obeying the angel's command when he had returned and found that his father was already dead (*pls 18-19*). Out of these seeds was to grow the tree from which the wood of the Cross would be taken.

21-5 The Queen of Sheba visits Solomon. While she was on her way to Jerusalem to visit Solomon, the Queen of Sheba had a revelation that the bridge over the little river Shiloh was built of the wood from which the Cross would be made, and she knelt before it in adoration (on the left of the fresco, *pl. 24*). The scene on the right shows her meeting with Solomon, to whom she imparted her revelation.

26 Removal of the Sacred Bridge. On being told by the Queen of Sheba that the bridge was sacred, Solomon had it removed. According to Schmarsow and Witting, Melozzo did some of the painting in this fresco, while Longhi cautiously suggests the name of Giovanni di Piemonte, the painter of an altarpiece in Città di Castello, signed and dated 1456, and similar in its rustic and noble treatment to the work of Piero della Francesca.

27-9 Annunciation of the death of the Virgin. I agree with Salmi that this fresco is not an Annunciation of the birth of Christ, but of the death of the Virgin. This is indicated by the palm the angel is holding in his hand instead of the lily (for the underlying concepts behind this choice of subject, see p. 19). The outstanding quality of this fresco shows it to be entirely by the hand of Piero.

30-1 Dream of Constantine. This episode precedes the *Victory of Constantine over Maxentius*, and represents the vision of Constantine, who was commanded by an angel to fight under the sign of the Cross. The ' nocturnal ' element in this fresco is thought to have been the inspiration of innumerable other works, especially Raphael's *Liberation of St Peter* in the Vatican. In this connection, and although Raphael did absorb something from Piero, Longhi's observation seems to me very just: ' the work of these artists, at the time it was executed, shows the assimilation of too many stylistic influences for such an ancestry to have a very precise significance '.

32-5 Victory of Constantine over Maxentius. This fresco, which is unfortunately in a dreadful condition, and with parts missing, represents the defeat of Maxentius at the Milvius Bridge by the triumphant Cross borne aloft by Constantine. In relation to this battle, as to the other between Heraclius and Chosroes, one must, I think, insist on the ' truth ' of Piero's vision; translating by means of his geometrical patterns the Roman soldiery and ornaments of war into an authentic fifteenth-century setting, where bodies of troops met on the open field of battle much as they did in Roman times. This confirms, once and for all, that Piero's abstraction is of a purely stylistic, rather than historical, order.

36-7 Torture of the Jew Judas. This scene too is ' true ', and of a contemporary reality. It represents a legend in which St Helen ordered the torture of the Jew Judas, the only person who knew where the Cross lay, after it had been buried following the death of

Christ. In this fresco, as in the *Removal of the Sacred Bridge*, Longhi sees the probable intervention of Giovanni di Piemonte.

38-45 Finding and proof of the Cross. Having learnt from Judas where the three Crosses were buried, St Helen had them disinterred (scene on the left) and was able to recognize the Cross of Christ by touching the body of a young man, who miraculously came back to life. The fresco is to a large extent by Piero's own hand.

46-9 Victory of Heraclius over Chosroes. The scene represented took place three hundred years later than the finding of the Cross. The Persian King Chosroes, who had captured the Cross in Jerusalem and made out of it an ornament for his throne, as well as the other symbols of the Passion, was conquered by the Emperor of the East, Heraclius. Much of the work of this fresco was done by assistants, and it becomes more and more difficult as we proceed from left to right to distinguish the authorship of the different parts. Compare the present reproduction of the bright head of the trumpeter, certainly by the hand of Piero (*pl. 48*), and the other head of the old warrior (*pl. 49*), where the careless, imprecise relationship between volume and colour range indicates the hand of an assistant.

50-4 Heraclius brings back the Cross to Jerusalem. This fresco depicts the humble entry of Heraclius into Jerusalem after the doors of the city had remained closed to the emperor bringing back the Cross in a lavish procession. Here too much of the work was done by assistants, though less than in the preceding fresco.

St Luke the Evangelist. Fresco. Rome, Santa Maria Maggiore, former Chapel of SS. Michele e Pietro. It has been ascribed to Piero by Longhi, who cautiously advanced the hypothesis that it was produced about the time Piero went to Rome during the pontificate of Nicholas V (who died in 1455), a journey attested by Vasari. He arrived at this conclusion because of the stylistic affinity between this fresco and the second stage of the Arezzo frescoes. Although Longhi himself also argued that Piero might equally have painted *St Luke* during the journey undertaken in 1459, for which there is certain documentary evidence, yet it seems to me that the first hypothesis is the more readily acceptable, both because it would confirm Vasari's information and because in my opinion this is without doubt an earlier work than the last of the Arezzo frescoes, and closer in style to the *The Queen of Sheba visits Solomon* and the *Victory of Constantine over Maxentius*. It was after the time of these frescoes, and possibly also of the *Prophet* on the right, that the journey to Rome may have occurred. This journey would also mark the passage from the first Arezzo period, when nearly all the work was by Piero's own hand, to the second stage, with its far greater use of assistants, as could be expected with Piero's increased fame and the consequently greater amount of work he had to undertake.

55 St Mary Magdalene. Fresco. Arezzo, Cathedral. By its style this fresco belongs to the same period as the last Arezzo frescoes, that is, 1455-60. It was recently restored by Leonetto Tintori.

56-7 Resurrection of Christ. Fresco. Borgo San Sepolcro, Town Hall. Datable to the time of the Arezzo frescoes, and earlier than the *St Augustine Polyptych*, this work was almost certainly executed after Piero's return from Rome. Vasari calls this Piero's masterpiece: ' considered the best of the works which are in that city, and of all his works '.

Hercules. Removed fresco. Boston, Gardner Collection. This painting was taken to Boston in 1906. It was originally in a house belonging to Piero in Borgo San Sepolcro. The figure was at one time full-length, and it is not known when it was cut down to its present dimensions by the removal of the lower part.

St Julian. Fresco. Museo di Borgo San Sepolcro. This fragment was discovered in 1954 in the former church of Sant'Agostino, Borgo. It is generally thought to be by the hand of Piero, although Salmi has certain reservations. It is datable to the period of the Arezzo frescoes.

St Apollonia. On panel. New York, Lehman Collection. It was published by Lehman in the catalogue of the collection, then by Lionello Venturi and finally by Longhi in the second edition of his monograph, when he suggested that it formed a part of the *St Augustine Polyptych*, which has not yet been entirely reconstructed. Longhi himself argued against this suggestion in his third edition, on the grounds that in *St Apollonia* the light falls from the left, whereas in all the panels of the *St Augustine Polyptych* it comes from the other side. He concluded his argument as follows: ' Given the fact... that the three small panels are of equal dimensions (*St Apollonia, St Monica* and an *Augustinian Saint* formerly in the Liechtenstein Collection) and that they probably all came from the same place, one may suppose that *St Apollonia* appeared in another altar, or at least another predella, of Piero's situated in the same church but on the opposite side. No third explanation can be envisaged, for we cannot charge Piero with lack of attention in executing a work which, in order to be a single whole, could not contravene the principle of unity of form in any aspect. ' This painting should probably be dated around 1460, as it is close in style to the last Arezzo period, and especially to the *St Mary Magdalene* in the cathedral (*pl. 55*).

58-60 St Augustine Polyptych. (For the plan of this altarpiece, see illustration on p. 37). On panel. Lisbon, Museum (*St Augustine, pls 58, 60*), London, National Gallery (*St Michael Archangel*, illustration on p. 25), New York, Frick Collection (*St John the Evangelist*, illustration on p. 25), Milan, Museo Poldi Pezzoli (*St Nicholas*

Schematic reconstruction of the St Augustine Polyptych

of *Tolentino*, pl. 59), Vienna, former Galerie Liechtenstein (*St Monica* and *Augustinian Saint*), New York, Rockefeller Collection (*Crucifixion*). Piero was commissioned to paint this altarpiece by the chapter of the church of Sant'Agostino in Borgo San Sepolcro in 1454, on the understanding that he would complete it within eight years, but it was not in fact paid for by the donors until 1469. Reconstruction of the altarpiece was undertaken independently by Millar Meiss in 1941 ('A Documented Altarpiece by Piero della Francesca', *The Art Bulletin*, March 1941) and by Longhi in the second edition of his monograph (1942), bringing together the three Saints in Milan, London and New York, the Liechtenstein and Rockefeller panels and the Lehman *St Apollonia* (see above). On the discovery in 1947 of the Lisbon *St Augustine*, Longhi made a final reconstruction in the third edition of his work (omitting the Lehman *St Apollonia*) and only the central panel and two saints in the predella are now missing. With regard to the subjects of the missing parts, as early as 1942 Longhi had assumed that the panel representing a saint, which had not yet been found, was *St Augustine*, and this supposition was shown to be correct by the finding of the Lisbon panel. He also assumed that the central panel represented the Virgin, as would be usual above the *Crucifixion* in the lower predella.

The polyptych was certainly dismembered before 1832, when Mancini (*Istruzione storico pittorica per visitare le chiese e i palazzi di Città di Castello. Appendice... delle più eccellenti tavole di San Sepolcro*) noticed in the choir of the nunnery church of Santa Chiara, in San Sepolcro, formerly Sant'Agostino, ' certain small painted panels, some of which seemed to be by the hand of Piero della Francesca'; these were probably the Liechtenstein and Rockefeller panels. According to Meiss, the polyptych was painted during the 1460s, but Longhi is inclined to date it earlier because its earliest sections (*St John the Evangelist* or *St Andrew* in the Frick Collection) are close in style to the later parts of the *Polyptych of the Misericordia*. In my opinion, these sections (the saints in the second row) are datable to the years around 1460, at the time of the payment made by the Brotherhood of the Misericordia to Marco di Benedetto, Piero's brother (1462, see above), and I fully accept the theory put forward by Meiss.

61-6 Perugia Polyptych. On panel. Perugia, Pinacoteca. Depicts the *Virgin and Child surrounded by St Antony, St John the Baptist, St Francis and St Elisabeth*; in the top panel is the *Annunciation* (*pls 62-3*), in the predella three Miracles of *St Francis* (*pl. 65*), *St Antony* (*pl. 66*) and *St Elizabeth*, and in two medallions *St Clare* and *St Agatha*. It was formerly in the church of Sant'Antonio delle Monache in Perugia. Datable to the 1460s.

67-70 Diptych of the Dukes of Montefeltro. On panel. Florence, Uffizi. On the reverse side of the portraits (*Federigo da Montefeltro, pl. 67; Battista Sforza, pl. 68*) are the *Triumphs* of the two dukes (*pls 69-70*). The work was dated by Cinquini (' Piero della Francesca a Urbino e i ritratti degli Uffizi ', *L'Arte*, 1906) to the year 1465, on the evidence of an ode by Ferrabò. It passed to the Medici in 1631 with the estate of the Della Rovere family.

71-2 Virgin and Child with angels. On panel. Williamstown, Mass., A. and J. Clark Institute. This appeared in the salerooms about 1925 and later came into the possession of the Williamstown Institute. It was published in 1930 by Gnoli (' Una tavola sconosciuta di Piero della Francesca ', *Dedalo*, 1930) and dated by him to about 1470, a date I believe we must substantially accept. Longhi, however, dates it a few years earlier.

73-4 Sinigallia Madonna. On panel. Urbino, Galleria Nazionale delle Marche. This painting came from the church of Santa Maria delle Grazie in Sinigallia. Of the same date as the Williamstown *Virgin and Child with angels* (*pls 71-2*).

75-6 Nativity. On panel. London, National Gallery. This painting reached the National Gallery in 1874, after successive sales, from the artist's family. It clearly belongs to the last period of Piero's style, close to the *Brera Altarpiece*.

77-80 Brera Altarpiece. On panel. Milan, Pinacoteca di Brera. This altarpiece represents the Virgin enthroned, surrounded by four angels and St John the Baptist, St Bernardine, St Jerome (on the left) and St Francis, St Peter the Martyr, and St Andrew (on the right). Federigo da Montefeltro is shown in act of prayer. It was formerly in the Church of San Bernardino in Urbino. Judging by the ages of the Montefeltros as they are shown here (much older than in the Uffizi diptych) and by the figure of St Peter the Martyr in whom, according to Ricci, is portrayed Luca Pacioli (born about 1445 and here at least thirty years of age), one may suppose the date of execution to be about 1475, a date which is in line with Piero's stylistic development. Pedro Berruguete did some of the painting of this altarpiece (he was documented as being present in Urbino in 1477), especially the duke's hands and the helmet on the ground next to him (Longhi).

2

4

5

6

7

11

15

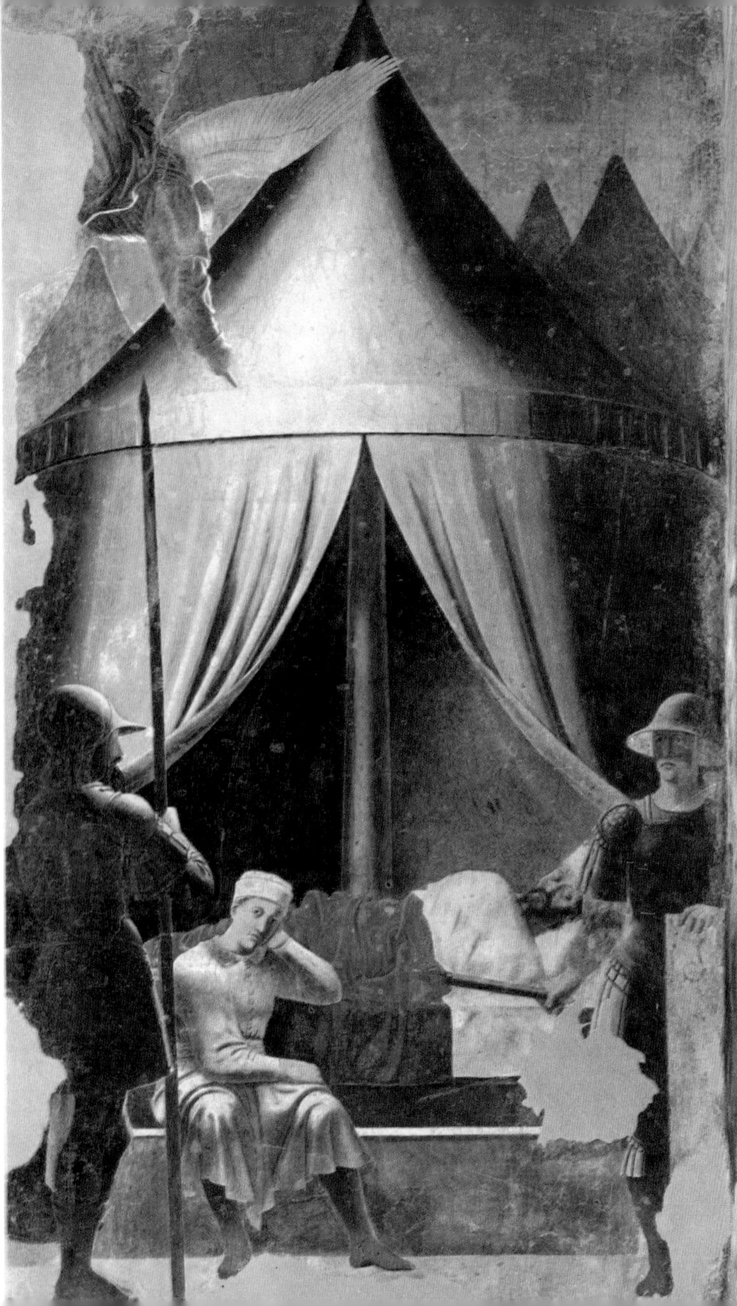

31

3

58

61

CLARVS INSIGNI VEHITVR TRIVMPHO ·
QVEM PAREM SVMMIS DVCIBVS PERHENNIS ·
FAMA VIRTVTVM CELEBRAT DECENTER ·
SCEPTRA TENENTEM ~

QVE MODVM REBVS TENVIT SECVNDIS ·
CONIVGIS MAGNI DECORATA RERVM ·
LAVDE GESTARVM VOLITAT PER ORA ·
CVNCTA VIRORVM ⁓